Cricki
Leaks

Cricki Leaks

The Secret Ashes Diaries

Tyers & Beach

First published in the UK in 2011 by John Wisden & Co
An imprint of Bloomsbury Publishing Plc
36 Soho Square, London W1D 3QY
www.wisden.com
www.bloomsbury.com

ISBN 978 1 4081 5240 9

A CIP catalogue record for this book is available from the British Library.

This book is produced using paper that is made from wood grown
in managed, sustainable forests. It is natural, renewable and
recyclable. The logging and manufacturing processes conform
to the environmental regulations of the country of origin.

Printed and bound in Great Britain by MPG Books Limited.

10 9 8 7 6 5 4 3 2 1

CrickiLeaks

EDITORS' NOTE

What follows is the most explosive* collection of cricketing diaries ever to see the light of day.

It has not been possible to verify the provenance of every dusty journal or grubby memory stick to have passed through our hands. However, each text has been carefully examined by scientists at the Trevor-Roper Institute using the very latest forensic techniques, including holding the paper up to the window to look for watermarks, doing a spell-check and, on one occasion, even looking something up on an "internet".

Although our sources must remain anonymous, we wish to extend particular thanks to the brave men and women of the Sydney Airport baggage handling service. Without their enquiring spirit and generosity with other people's property, the world of cricket would be a poorer place.

*not literally

THE SECRET ASHES DIARIES

The Abominable Showman

W.G. Grace

Southampton Dock, September 18th 1892

A day of near perpetual motion! The steamship to Australia leaves this evening and there were multitudinous affairs to put in order before traversing the globe to give the convict the sound thrashing that is his due.

To Bristol, and a century before lunch. However, my enjoyment of the innings was severely compromised on two counts. Firstly, an uppity young left-arm bowler laboured under the misapprehension that he had bowled me out on three separate occasions – and had the cheek to ask "how is that?" of the umpire each time. I impressed upon him the obvious truth that it was the local sou'easter which had uprooted my middle stump, rather than the ball as he had erroneously surmised; and ensured that the breeze could not engender further confusion by nailing the bails onto the stumps with a mallet. I fancied I detected a show of dissent on behalf of the fellow, and had no alternative but to administer a thorough beating with the mallet and relieve him of his fee for the match. I tenderised and fined the umpire too, *pour encourager les autres*.

Worse, a member of the crowd was taken unwell and I was obliged to attend to the wretched man. I make no pleasantry whatsoever when I say that the life of the parish doctor would be quite tolerable were it not for the constant demands of the ghastly populace. Is there anything more weak and uncricketly than the ill? However, each of us must bear his burden, and I agreed to examine the fellow down by the third man boundary.

He was a particularly shambolic individual, groaning and clutching at his hindquarters, which were evidently giving him considerable pain. It was immediately clear to a physician of my experience that he was suffering from some unmentionable nonsense in the downstairs area. This I attributed to the wrong sort of foods, not drinking enough beer and, as it turned out after questioning the creature, not playing enough cricket. I diagnosed haemorrhoids, prescribed a pottage of mercury to be applied to the fundament and strongly advised some assiduous work on his hitting to leg. I admonished him: "Young man, they have come to see me bat, not your bowel," and returned to the wicket, where I scored a further 150 before declaring and hailing a hansom cab to take me to the port.

I stopped en route at Lord's and negotiated my tour fee with Lord Sheffield, who is nominally in charge of the tour. There was an unfortunate incident on the road to Southampton when the horse pulling my baggage collapsed dead under the weight of the enormous bag of money. However, I was not disheartened and, after building a small bonfire at the side of the roadway from the now-useless carriage, I fashioned a simple but hearty meal out of the deceased equine. Restored, I now await to board the ship and travel onward to glory.

Justin Langer

Secret location for dossier research, October 18th 2010

A few thoughts on the English team, based on my experience of playing in England, my own observations from my Test career but mainly some stuff that I overheard Steve Waugh saying on the golf course when I was caddying for him this morning.

The key thing to remember about your English cricketer is that he is, above all, English. Put another way, he is not Australian – with all that entails. Your classic English cricketer will not look you in the eye, has terrible body language, bad teeth and slightly small feet. He is vulnerable to the short ball, feeds only at night, and would sell his mates down the river for a gin and tonic. He hates dogs, plays the viola and sent our ancestors to their death at Gallipoli while he sat reading poetry and twirling his moustache. This team is full of that exact sort of Englishman.

To be more specific:

ANDREW STRAUSS: Solid guy. Left-hander. Get him out caught or bowled. Look to get him out early.

ALASTAIR COOK: Solid left-hander. Guy. Look to get him bowled, caught, leg before. Also run out or stumped. Possible candidate for handled the ball, timed out or obstructing the field. Look to get him out early.

JONATHAN TROTT: Confusing one. Possible pussy? But not English. Non-English pussy. Is this possible? More information needed: could be trap. Vulnerable to 95 MPH leg-cutter on good length. Look to get him out early.

KEVIN PIETERSEN: Play on ego. Starve him of oxygen of publicity, like a terrorist. Can get unhappy when he is not happy.

PAUL COLLINGWOOD: Do not get him out early.

IAN BELL: Right-hander. Was NOT in *American Pie* movie franchise, despite rumours. Could be vulnerable to light-hearted on-field banter such as, "We're going to burn down your house and kill all your friends and family."

MATT PRIOR: Big mouth. Big pussy? Horny thought.

STUART BROAD: Head could go down if not winning, or if hit on head with cricket bat in ambush.

GRAEME SWANN: Key. Morally suspect? Lure with honey trap? Or honey? Possibly vulnerable to attack from swarm of killer bees?

JIMMY ANDERSON: Bowler. Reformed pussy. Prefers winning to losing. Look to hit balls bowled by him, or block depending on situation.

STEVE FINN: Tall. Look to bite on ankle?

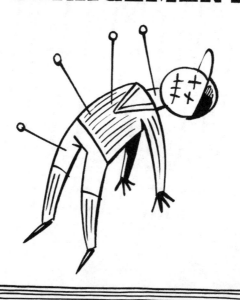

Kirk Russell
England physiotherapist

Loughborough, October 15th 2010

Final preparations for the winter tour to Australia are going well, although I have some concerns about one or two fringe players. On today's fitness exercise at the outdoor athletics track, Samit Patel ordered a taxi to take him the last two laps. This would be bad enough in itself; however, telling the driver to take him "via the nearest Nandos, innit" simply will not do. In my professional opinion, chicken nuggets are not "isotonic", as Samit believes. And pausing during a timed beep test to order a pizza seems unlikely to convince management that he will be able to perform under pressure in a big-game situation.

October 16th

While Tim Bresnan is a whole-hearted player in a lot of respects, what you might call the mental side of his physical conditioning needs work. He is extremely sensitive to perceived jibes about his size: in this morning's gym session, I told him to consider some work on the hamstring and gluteus muscles to increase power in the delivery stride. 45 minutes later, he was still locked in the lavatory sobbing: "You said my bum looks big in this tracksuit – how could you?" It was only by agreeing that the whole squad could work for an hour on their "Sprinkler Dance" – and sending James Anderson out for a bunch of flowers – that we managed to coax him out at all. While there has not, to the best of my knowledge, been a Yorkshire fast bowler with anorexia in the past, we should keep an eye on this.

October 17th

Called AF and told him we need to talk about Kevin. Stuart Broad's recent forays into the world of topless modelling have caused great amusement among most of the lads, but Kevin has reacted very negatively to (in his words) "a younger pin-up coming along and turning everyone's heads". He has taken to working obsessively in the aerobics/dance studio with his shirt off, shouting "I've still got it" and watching *Black Swan* over and over again on his iPad.

While a bit of healthy competition between the boys is great, I think today's episode went too far. Kevin found out that Stuart was on his way to a photo shoot and substituted the baby oil that Stuart uses for his pectorals with linseed. With a gruelling winter schedule coming up, we could scarcely afford to lose a key member of the bowling attack with a grade-two irritated nipple, and this injury will need careful monitoring.

Steve Waugh
Aged 10¾

Sydney, March 12th 1976

I looked around my classmates with disbelief. Where was their passion, their strength of character, their desire to be the best Year Five Australian History Class we could possibly be?

Their happy faces were like a knife to my heart punching me in the gut.

The teacher had told us we could vote on the end-of-term school trip and, showing an incredible lack of focus and determination, they had all voted for Uncle Bongo's Kangaroo Korner.

Sydney's leading petting zoo. Unbelievable.

We have a massive year of under-11s cricket coming up and we were going to work on the mental side of our game by cuddling orphan kangaroos? Say we were six down for spit in a big game, would we draw strength from knowing that we knew how to rub a furry tummy? Or the role of the kangaroo's pouch in the birth of our great nation? It made my blood boil.

A year ago, I had lead the class on an orienteering expedition around the Waugh back garden. It was a fantastic bonding exercise. And so what if some cry-babies were locked in the shed for a night or two or a couple of people were bitten by snakes? It made us the under-10 cricket outfit we were last year. Even Mark enjoyed it: he won two weeks' pocket money betting on which of the girls would cry first. If you're reading, Sally Ferguson, why don't you grow a pair, eh?

Kangaroo Korner. Even the name made me angry. *Kangaroo Korner*. I had always hated the letter "K", a sneaky, lazy letter that would be a "C" if it had a bit more strength of character. A Pommie of a letter.

I had argued we should go to the Anzac Wall of Brave Heroes and Bloody Good Mates. It's the best visitor attraction in Sydney bar none, a superb day out for any family. It commemorates great Australians who came out fighting when their backs were to the wall. Simple. Powerful. You spend a day standing with your back up against the wall and feeling proud of our country.

Believe it or not, some of my classmates said they found "just standing up straight against a wall" for six hours "boring". I told them there was loads more to it than that: you also got to listen to stories of great Australians doing things like scrapping when the chips were down, never giving up and showing intensity no matter what the situation. They wouldn't listen.

I knew I had to take action. As soon as I got on the coach I started to mentally disintegrate the driver. "Mate, there's no way you're fit to drive this bus," I said. The teacher was furious and I had to sit at the front next to her for the whole journey to Kangaroo Korner. And as a punishment, they never even let me pet the furry tummies of the little baby roos. One day, I am going to shove that down their throats.

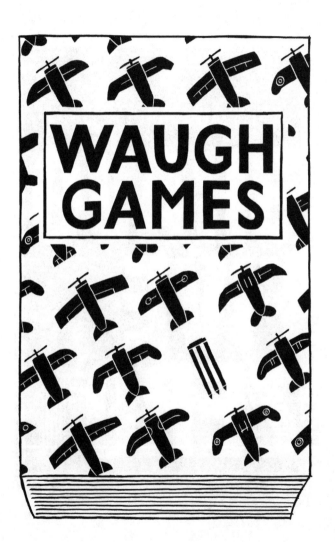

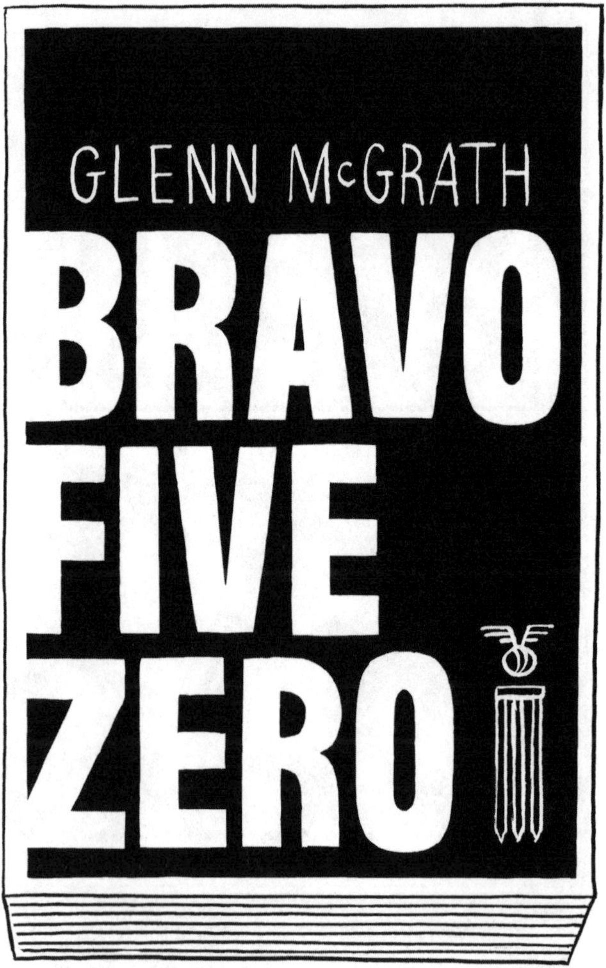
GLENN McGRATH
BRAVO
FIVE
ZERO

Glenn McGrath

Sydney, October 15th 2010

The Ashes are nearly here and it's going to be a busy time for me with my predictions. I've been rushed off my feet gathering runes, entrails and the like ahead of the series and preparing my tarot tent at all the Test venues. People think that it's all beer and skittles, just a bit of a laugh going, "Oh yeah, 5-0 mate" every time the Poms show up. Well, it's not. Maybe if I was some sort of hack like that Jonathan Cainer of the Pom *Daily Mail* it would be. But seeing into the future is a serious business and you have to know what you're messing with. It's like bowling an off-cutter to a left-hander if you haven't softened him up with the rib-tickler and put the hard word on him first: you are trifling with forces beyond your control, and that is not something you want to be doing. Just look at poor young Mitchell: one of our most promising practitioners of the black arts as was, and now he couldn't predict an ice cream will melt on the bonnet of a ute during the Narromine hot season.

October 22nd

Still not had any luck persuading young Brett to throw his lot in with me. Mystic Glenn McGrath and Gypsy Rose Lee: we could take the clairvoyant world by storm. But Brett's got his musicals and his men's outfitters and

I suppose I have to respect that. I won't give up, though, and he'll come round in the end. I have foreseen it. And if I have to lock him in a dressing-room overnight, get the Ouija board out and get old Merv Hughes done up in a white sheet to put the frighteners on him, then sorry Binger, that's how it's going to be.

October 26th

Devastated to read about the death of Paul the Octopus who did such awesome predictive work during the soccer World Cup in Germany. Obviously, I foresaw it was going to happen before it did, but when any member of the clairvoyant community – be they human or seafood – passes to the other side, it is always a sad day. I knew Paul a little, he had an incredible gift for prediction and he was a hell of a useful left-armer – and right-armer as well, come to that. My heart just goes out to Paul's family, friends and other *Fusbalpredichtopussen* everywhere. He's gone to the great 5–0 hammering in the sky, or ocean I guess in his belief system, but he will not be forgotten.

Fred Spofforth
The Demon Bowler

Kennington, August 27th 1882, late at night
Slipping in and out of sleep. Excited about doing battle with the English tomorrow. The Doctor looms large in my dreams. There is nothing I would not give to bowl out that pompous Pom.

August 28th
I awake. I am bathed in sweat, twitching, heart racing – like a corpulent Sheila in a piemongers. I have had a night of dreams so vivid, so intense that I swear they are as real as this pencil, this paper and this refreshing glass of beer and hunk of raw beefsteak with which I make my morning repast.

I dreamed I awoke and, in a trance as if still asleep, left my team-mates sleeping in the bunk room. Soon I was outside in the warm (for this frigid country) night air. I did not know where I was going, yet I was not lost either. A sure, cold certainty gripped at me, like it does when I am about to stick a fast one up the hooter of a tailender in one of those stripy caps the Pom toffs have.

Presently, I find myself standing at a crossroads. In my mind, I know it is the junction of Harleyford Road and Kennington Lane and yet at the same time it is not there, nor anywhere in this world either. It is suddenly very cold and I shiver, pulling my koala pelt nightshirt around my body. The place is as empty and barren as an Englishman's heart.

Fear grips me and I sense I am not alone. I turn, and a figure appears. A male of age almost impossible to place, broad, bearded. His face is unholy white, his eyes like two dot balls in a scorer's book, piercing into my soul.

"I hear you desire to be the greatest bowler that ever drew breath? To rout the English on their own land? To burn your name into legend forever?"

His voice is deep and without pity.

"Aw look," I say. "Well. Yes. Yes, I do."

"My price is simple," says the man – if man he be. "I ask only for your soul."

"Steady on, mate," I say.

"I am not for bargaining or idle chat," he roars. "Do you know who I am?"

"I can guess," I say to him. "You're the flaming Devil, ain't ya?"

"Well," says the Dark Lord. "So what if I am? I have no time for pleasantries; I am here to talk cricket, and I've got a bloody fortune on tomorrow's match. So here is my proposition, Fred Spofforth. You get bowling greatness; I get your immortal soul."

"I am not sure," I say.

"14 wickets in the match you shall take, the English will be destroyed and your name will ring out for ever more: The Demon. And I'll chuck in this little urn, if you like. It's got a burned stump in it, or something."

"Alright mate," I say. "You're on."

The Life
And
Loves
of a
He-Devil

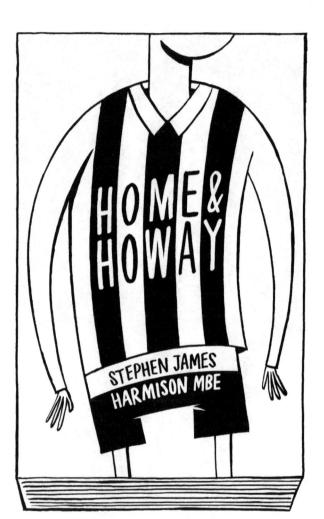

HOME & HOWAY

STEPHEN JAMES
HARMISON MBE

Steve Harmison

Brisbane, November 23rd 2006, 10:00 AM

I'm ready. I'm fresh; not worn out from bowling a load of overs in warm-up games that don't mean anything. People don't realise how much cricket has changed: maybe in the old days there was a lot of bowling day in, day out, but things are more sophisticated now with the science and everything like that. We'll play a bit of football for fitness, do a bit of work in the nets, some karate, bit of dodgeball, then watch videos.

Yesterday, we saw *Gladiator*. I like that bit where Russell Crowe has the little statues of his wife and son that he kisses before he goes into the arena. They say Test cricket is like being a modern gladiator, with the crowd and the duel between bowler and batter. And there being a lot of foreigners in it. Fortunately in this day and age, there's mobiles and internet and everything, so you don't have to carry tiny statues of your kids around when you go abroad. But the principle's the same: there's no better way for me to focus and get ready to go to war than talking to my little ones for a couple of hours.

This morning, I've been working on my positive visualisation. A lot of top sportsmen are using it these days, even big-money footballers. You visualise yourself in your mind achieving your goals: in my case I picture myself having a few beers with Freddie and the Aussie lads. It's definitely more enjoyable playing against a team you can have a laugh with. I think we're probably more like this Aussie team than any other international side: we play hard, sure, and we want to win, but that'll never get in the way of a few cold beers at the close of play. At the end of the day, the Aussies know that enjoyment is what it's really all about, and so do we. That's something that Fred's really brought to the team: I think he's going to be a great captain. He lets us express ourselves, whether it's through drinking games, flaming shots or just having a couple of quiet ones and talking about whatever.

Talking of team spirit in that dressing-room, people ask if we've focused for too long on celebrating the 2005 win. I think definitely not, no. If you ask any sportsman they will tell you that it's important to enjoy your success, you've earned it, you deserve it. Feel satisfied by it. Savour it, if you like. Reliving your past victories definitely makes you hungrier.

And I am hungry. It really pisses me off when people say I'm not. At breakfast this morning, I could have had Frosties: instead, I ordered brown toast with scrambled eggs. The eggs were a bit undercooked; I didn't care. I'm not a cry-baby. I could hear the *Rocky* theme tune in my head as I ate them. I think in the past my biggest failing as a cricketer has been trying too hard. I'm over that now. All I can see in my mind is that ball flying into Fred's big hands at slip and the crowd going wild.

Brisbane, November 23rd, 11:04 AM
Bugger.

Douglas Jardine

At sea, somewhere hot and hateful, September 23rd 1932
Still several weeks until we reach Australia, and we are
thoroughly bored of being cooped up on this ship. I dine
early and alone, as is my custom, and later perambulate
around the deck. There I am accosted by a most frightful
Australian female who appears to be suffering from sea
sickness, although the water is as flat as the sort of pitches
upon which the charlatan Bradman makes his runs. The
individual is clinging desperately to the gunwale like an
Australian Member of Parliament holding a flagon of
their insipid beer. Of course, this sort of cowardice is
bred into your Australian when they are but babes in
arms, and I tell her as much.

"Help me," says the wretched woman. "Young man,
could you possibly escort me back to my cabin? I am
afraid I feel most peculiar, strewth."

Fortuitously, I have with me my walking cane and
I am thus able to protect myself from the Antipodean
blackguard and no-doubt certain assault or robbery. I
rain upon her a tiny portion of the beatings that are her
due, and retire to my cabin. I never could abide nuns.

Sydney, or other such cesspit, December 1st
The Test match begins tomorrow, thus our Australian
hosts have organised a welcoming ceremony which,
to their unsophisticated minds, I imagine appears one

of considerable pomp and circumstance. I tolerate their salutations and speechifying with patient disdain, like a father being shown a worthless drawing by one of his least-favoured offspring. A small child approaches to present me with some sort of infantile flag or pennant, presumably for commemorative purposes. Fortunately, Larwood is watching closely for my signal and is able to fell the little bastard with a well-aimed bread roll before it can get too close. I instruct Larwood and Voce to distract the mob while I make good my escape.

Adelaide, or very possibly Hell, January 20th 1933
Australians, from the lowest born to what passes for the upper echelons, are indulging in their national pastime: whining and griping about me. And, sure enough, a telegram has arrived from London asking me to explain my actions during the Adelaide Test. I shall not. I am the representative in this country of the British Empire and His Majesty King George, and if I wish to go into Adelaide Zoo and defile a prize koala, I shall do so, and I shall answer to nobody but the Marylebone Cricket Club. Frankly, the creature was asking for it, and I should do the same again, national animal or not. I shall send it an ashtray later to smooth things over, and as far as I am concerned, that is the end of the matter.

Mike Gatting

Old Trafford, June 4th 1993

What a day. I knew it was going to be a tough one as soon as I got to the dining room and saw that Merv Hughes had beat me to the fried bread. He'd had the bear's share of that, the greedy fat Aussie sod, and there was hardly enough left to mop up my fourth fried egg. I was reduced to sticking my streaky unsmoked (unsmoked since the health kick – thanks for nothing, Dr Killjoy) between some bits of black pudding to fashion a makeshift sandwich. But that's international sport: you have to react to changing environments, think on your feet. At times like this, I always say to myself. "Gatt, firstly: think of that emergency Branston in your kitbag and b) at least we're not in Pakistan."

Hardly surprising then, that I didn't have the best day in the field, probably my blood sugar was low after the reduced breakfast. Athletes' bodies are not the same as ordinary people's and a disruption in your refuelling regime can really throw you out of kilter. I think I got over-hungry, like when you're over-tired and can't sleep, and I couldn't get anything down me for the rest of the morning's play. Even the hog roast I had the twelfth man bring on at drinks tasted funny, and I barely touched my second haunch of venison at lunch. Or the baked beans. Cheeseboard? Not for Gatt today. Yeah. That's how badly I was suffering. Even Beefy was sympathetic, in his way, and tried to cheer me up with a couple of pints and a listen of his favourite *Mrs Thatcher Sings The Hits of Elton John* cassette. It didn't do any good.

All in all, I was feeling pretty sorry for myself by the time I came out to bat. To be quite honest with you, I didn't know a lot about Shane Warne – I heard he could put away an XXXL Mighty Meaty in a pretty warm order, but other than that I was in the dark about his abilities. He was licking his lips as I took guard and I suppose it was the tiredness and the hunger but my vision sort of went blurry, like Tuffers said you go after one of his roll-ups, and with that bright blonde hair and that sweaty red face and the pink tongue sticking out, he looked more or less exactly like a sherry trifle. I'm partial to a bit of trifle and I was just thinking about getting after a really good one with a nice wafer biscuit or a couple of sausages to spoon it up with when he's ripped one and next thing I know I'm stumbling back to the pavilion in a sort of daze.

I got back to the dressing-room and they were all saying, "Jesus Christ, did you see that?" and I said: "Too right, they've got a bowler who can impersonate puddings at will," and I think if we're honest with ourselves we lost the series there and then.

Denis Compton

Highbury, September 26th 1936
No cricket to be had today, so I make my debut for the Arsenal against Derby County. Score a goal. At half-time, chatter turns to a rumour that the club has plans to sign a foreign player. And a Frenchman, at that! I cannot believe we will ever see the day, not at the Arsenal. After the match, a chap approaches me with a "business opportunity". Will I have my picture taken and printed in magazines etc with the words: "I am Denis Compton and I think these cigarettes are splendid – and very restorative to the lungs after a quick sprint up the left wing"? In exchange, I will receive a large bag of money. There seems to be no reason to say no.

Trent Bridge, June 11th 1938
Make my debut for England; score century against Australia. At lunch, a man comes and gives me an enormous suitcase full of money. Turns out, I am an enthusiastic consumer of Powdered Egg, and never fail to scoff down a great deal of it before going out to bat. Too right, I say. Hammond is glaring at me furiously. Perhaps he is not partial to the Powdered Egg?

London, September 2nd 1939
Score couple of centuries for Middlesex; pop over to Highbury where I stick the winner past Everton; sign

new "sponsorship agreement" in which I make it known that I simply never leave the house without a refreshing swig of Brylcreem. (Is that right?) Life seems to be going quite nicely, what with the cricket and the football and the saying I like things in exchange for the large amounts of money. What could possibly go wrong?

London, September 3rd 1939
Ah. Unfortunately, it would seem that we are at war with Germany. There is talk that football, cricket, and even possibly the large bags of pound notes for liking things might be on ice for a while.

Trent Bridge, June 14th 1948
Sorry haven't written for a while, was rather busy. Finally found diary again under enormous pile of cheques. Unbeaten overnight on 154 against Australia. Bradman does seem to take it all very seriously, doesn't he? Of slight concern: wake in night and trip over pile of gold bullion from friends at Brylcreem, hurting knee quite badly in the process. Sure it will be fine and, on the upside, my hair is immaculate. Do I get money for writing this?

Gemma Broad
Team England video analyst

Perth, December 20th 2010

Mike Hussey has already scored 195, DNB, 93, 52, 61 and 116 against us, and Andy Flower had asked me to put together a video package for the bowlers. I showed the lads some things I wanted to highlight, a possible weakness with Hussey's trigger movement to the shorter ball at around 86 MPH and a hint of a crooked bat against the one that comes back from outside off once the ball is between 50 and 65 overs old.

The session was a bit frustrating, to be honest. I turned around for one second and Swanny had grabbed one of my video cameras and started "making a pilot for a hilarious sketch show that we should deffo pitch to ITV4." Jimmy was only interested in studying the different types of moisturiser and zinc sunscreen Hussey uses and speculating about the effects they might have on his skin ahead of some big modelling gig for *What Boy?* magazine he's got coming up. Tim Bresnan thought he saw a Battenberg cake in the crowd but we couldn't get the resolution high enough on the freeze-frame so he lost interest. I won't pretend it's easy; but I do get to work with the England women's team as well, so it's nice to see that adults can benefit from what I do, as well as children.

December 21st

Stuart's been really down since he had to fly home with his injury so I made him a little highlights package of some of his best Ashes moments to try and cheer him up. There's a nice clip of him calling Shane Watson "a tool" in the first Test, and then one of him glaring aggressively at Michael Clarke in Adelaide and making a "tosser" gesture behind his back where his wrist position is just perfect.

He studies his tapes really carefully; he's always trying to work out the most intimidating distance to stare at a batsman from, varying his angle of tantrum, what's the perfect swearword to deliver. He never stops thinking about all aspects of his game. I've got some footage of him up before the match referee recently and I know Andy Flower is keen to get him to think about his head position so he looks a bit more sorry when he's apologising to Ranjan Madugalle. It's little things like dipping the head and looking up with the eyes – Flower is always drilling it into him: "Think about your Princess Dianas" – that can make the difference between a slap on the wrist and half a match fee.

Ashley Giles

Adelaide, November 30th 2006

Thought I did okay at Brisbane, stuck a tidy one-fer in my back bin and put my hand up with the bat, but that hasn't stopped a lot of people talking about Monty. Don't get me wrong, Monty is a good lad and a fine bowler, but is he what we in the Fletcher era refer to as "a five-tool player"? In layman's terms, that means can he do five different things. Can he bat? Can he bowl? Can he field? Is he good value in the 19th hole? Is he a hundred and ten percenter?

The jury's out on Monty, he's probably a three-to-four tooler: over five Tests, is that enough? He's arguably a hundred and ten percenter, but even when you multiply his other three, three-and-a-half tools by 110, are you getting the bang for your buck that an Ashley Giles gives you? That's not for Ash to answer.

Adelaide, Second Test, day three, December 3rd

Obviously, some people would say that dropping Ricky Ponting when he was on 30-odd was a setback. But would, say – picking an example at random – would, say, Monty Panesar have caught that? Tricky one. I'm going to say no. In fact, maybe it's turned out a lot worse: Monty's dropped it, it's bounced off his foot, rebounded and hit him in the face. He's in agony, Harmy's run over to check he's okay, he's tripped over Monty and done his leg in; it's a Simon Jones situation all over again. Harmy can't handle travelling to Edinburgh twice a week for the rehab on his knee, he starts drinking, he loses the plot and next thing you know he's rattling around the place in a wheelchair, shouting and ranting, like a Geordie version of Tom Cruise in *Born on the Fourth of July*. To be fair, I'd argue we got off lightly.

Adelaide, Second Test, day five, December 5th

Shane Warne this, Shane Warne that, Shane Warne spun us to victory, blah, blah, blah. Don't get me wrong, Shane is a special talent, although his methods are definitely a bit *obvious* for your spin bowling purist. Turning it this way, turning it the other, then the flipper and the zooter. It's effective, in a showy sort of way.

But we could all be hogging the limelight with our variety if we wanted, couldn't we? The Spinners' Union is getting a bit tired of it, to be fair. I'm chairman next season, since Ian Salisbury stood down to spend more time with his tomato plants, and I'm tabling a motion about all these so-called "mystery spinners" with their so-called "mystery balls". Ooh, look at me, I took a wicket with my mystery ball. Fairground showmen, I call them. The whole point of having a mystery ball is that you don't bowl it: it's a deterrent. Like, what would be the sense in Britain having a nuclear deterrent if we went and bombed Russia or whoever back to the Stone Age? I reckon it's a cheap trick, and we, as an international spin bowling community, should be better than that.

ASHLEY GILES
OMISSION: IMPOSSIBLE

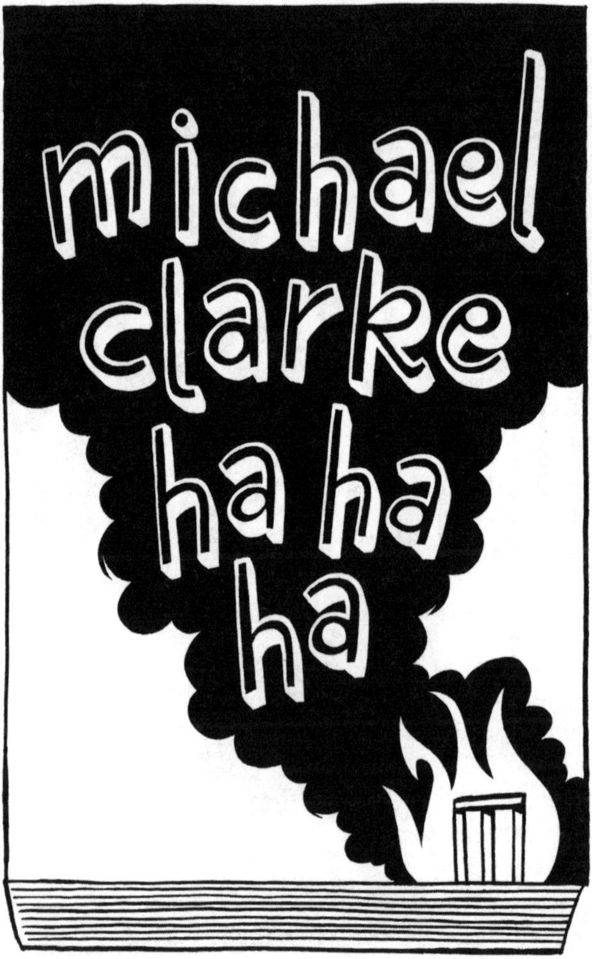
michael
clarke
ha ha
ha

Michael Clarke

Adelaide, Second Test, day four, December 6th 2010

6:15 PM

Not a good evening. Got out to Kevin Pietersen with five balls left of the day, then straight into the rooms to face Ricky. Ricky might not be the most intellectual guy, but he's got a hell of a vocabulary on him. I defended myself as best I could ("Not my face! Not my face!") for getting out, and also for my Tweet saying I was sorry for not walking as soon as I hit the ball. I guess I'm part of the new generation of Australian cricketers, a modern young guy if you like, and I needed to share how I feel. Is it so wrong to feel? To express? To show a bit of vulnerability?

7:15 PM

Ricky just texted and asked me to come to a meeting.

9:45 PM

That didn't go very well at all.

10:45 PM

Just about stopped shaking. Ricky had arranged for Steve Waugh, Allan Border and Ian Chappell to come and talk to me about saying sorry for not walking. Words were used, not nice words. Words like "un-Australian". "Metrosexual". Even "gallah". It's not much fun being shouted at for two hours and 30 minutes. Especially when you've got a film première to attend.

1:35 AM
Woke up after terrible nightmare. Dreamed I was driving a really nice Ferrari down the highway with Lara back by my side. But then I went to kiss her and she turned into my primary school teacher and then Dean Jones ran in front of the car. I hit the brakes and swerved to avoid him. The car rolled over. I got out, I was alright – but Lara had vanished. The car was a write-off. Dean said, "What are you going to do now?" and I said, "I guess I'll walk," and he totally lost it. His face turned into a wolf's and I tried to put moisturiser on it for him and then he started chasing me and trying to kill me. Alfie Langer was sitting on his shoulders cackling.

4:55 AM
Still lying here trying to work out what my dream means.

Keith Richards

Somewhere, June (?) 1972 (?)
I don't know how the hell we got here.

Last time I looked we were at Madison Square Garden, but here definitely isn't there. Mick told me he wanted to go to Lord Somebody's to see a guy called Bob Massie who was doing some incredible things. I'd never heard of this Massie. I guessed he must be some guy from the Delta or maybe out of Nashville or something, but I couldn't stand the thought of Mick knowing about a player I didn't so I said sure why not, and we just rolled onto the jet.

I look around the place, it's some sort of open-air arena and Mick, as is his way, is immediately right at home. He's charming and smarming with a lot of serious-looking, dignified establishment cats in matching red-and-yellow ties. The butterfly on a wheel crowd, if you know what I mean. I turn to the one sitting next to me, a guy with a far-out set of lambchop whiskers, and tell him I don't like the atmosphere here. Too heavy, man.

"Very heavy indeed," he agrees. "The ball will be swinging like nobody's business. Of course, a session *can* be more exciting in these gloomy conditions."

"I know what you're saying," I tell him. "The sunshine bores the daylights out of me, man."

We both just sort of zone out for a while and when I start to focus again, I remember I've got some serious gear with me. It's burning a hole in my pocket, and I'm wondering where I can scratch an itch.

My new friend offers me a gin and tonic, which goes down okay apart from there being tonic in it, and it only seems polite to share what I'm holding.

"From Pakistan," I tell him. "I don't cut it, either."

"Well, absolutely not," he says. "Certainly not before June."

I get up to find the john when a heavy comes over and says, "please take your seat during play, sir." I've met some mean bastards during my multiple run-ins with the authorities but I reckon this guy might be the most miserable of the lot.

I figure I better do what he says and I notice Mick's hissing over at me. "Keith, you're embarrassing me," he says. "I'm very sorry about my friend, Mr Evans."

"Godfrey, please," says the cat with the whiskers. "And it's quite alright. I was just saying to Keith here that he must join the MCC."

"That's like totally unfair, man," says Mick. "I've been on the waiting list for years."

"Never mind, Mick," I say. "You can't always get what you want, you know?"

"I'm sure your turn will come sooner or later," says whiskers and the two of us go off to see about that Pakistani.

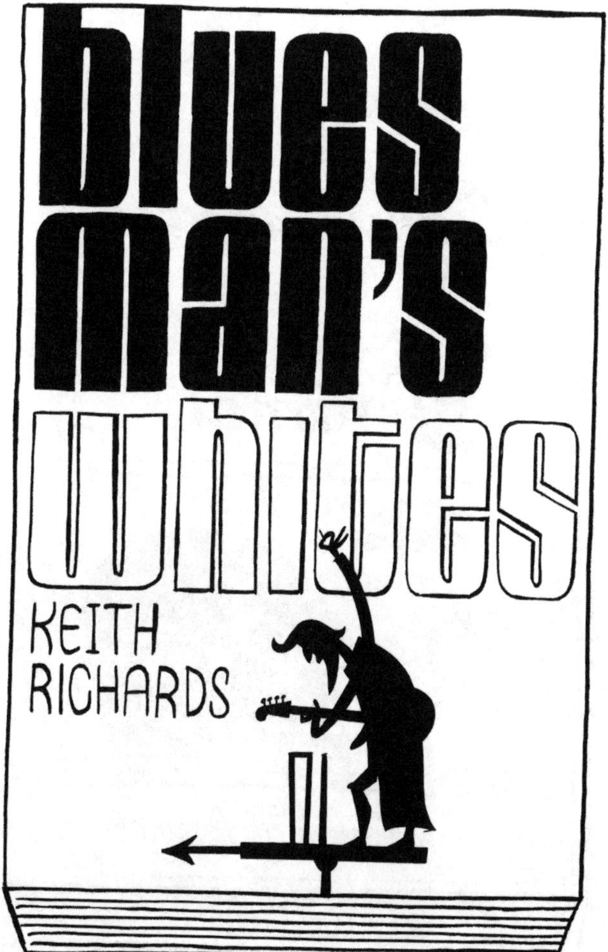
blues
man's
whites
KEITH
RICHARDS

My Team-mates And Other Animals

The Nawab of Pataudi

The Nawab of Pataudi

Worcester, August 7th 1932

A telegram arrives from London offering me a place on Jardine's tour of Australia. I am most considerably uncertain as to whether I should go, for there are pressing matters to attend to here in my beloved adopted home of Worcestershire. My plans to build the world's most magnificent and lavish polo ground in Droitwich Spa take up considerable reserves of time, as do my efforts to track and shoot a good specimen of the indigenous Hick's badger.

While I confess I am curious to see what sort of people and vegetation grow in the Antipodes, my understanding of the native is that he is not a keen player of polo, and that some of the poorer inhabitants did not even attend university! Of course, this may be merely an unkind rumour.

In addition, I find Jardine to be the most frightful oik and abhor his theories of bowling the ball at the batsman's body, to say nothing of his wearing a Harlequin cap rather than a much more sensible big turban with all diamonds in it.

Sydney, December 6th

A day of mixed emotions: I recorded my maiden Test century, 102 off 327 balls. Had I not taken so many risks in my innings, I might have scored more. I was just starting to feel set.

When we came to bowl, Jardine instructed me to field at short leg as his horny-handed agents of destruction unleashed their barrage of beastliness. I declined.

"I see His Highness is a conscientious objector," he sneered.

My retort was rather brilliant, though I say so myself: "I tell you who wasn't a conscientious objector – your mater, last night," I said to him.

Angered, Jardine banished me to field at third man. "I tell you who was also keen on a third man," I began, but Jardine told Larwood to look at me in a threatening manner and I decided that discretion ought to be the better part of valour.

Melbourne, December 30th
Quite content fielding on the boundary today, where I was able to study an extraordinary bipedal, hairy mammal that I took to be some sort of lower primate. I was just about to bag it with my blunderbuss, thinking its pelt would look quite splendid in the canasta room of Pataudi Towers, Kidderminster, when it was pointed out to me that this was not, despite appearances, wildlife, but rather a female member of the Australian crowd.

When I told Jardine, he was livid. He said that my failure to at least pepper the specimen with buckshot was tantamount to treason. I do not expect I shall play for him again.

Ted Dexter

Headingley, June 7th 1989

As England Selector, I make it a rule never to talk to the players. This is not, contrary to popular belief, because they are yobs with no manners, no appreciation of the finer things in life and absolutely zero *savoir faire*. Rather, it is so I can make a full and fair judgement of their abilities without being swayed by personal feelings, be they negative or – theoretically – even positive.

However, I did chat to one extremely impressive young man today at Headingley, a shortish, rugged left-hander with a steely manner, and I am certain that he should be rushed into the England team ahead of the first Test.

Headingley, June 8th

Irritating. My left-hander from yesterday goes by the name of Border and is captaining the opposition. Rotten luck once again – I expect Pluto must be regressing in Saturn, very likely as a result of the horrid smog in that part of the solar system.

Trent Bridge, August 10th

Have dropped rather a brick. I arrived at Trent Bridge yesterday and immediately ran into Gower in the gents. Couldn't quite face another soul-searching chat about the state of what passes for the England cricket team, and I fancied he was rather of the same mind. However, I can't bear an awkward silence so I started telling him about an excellent weekend I'd had golfing down in the West Country, and recommended a very good hotel in the Torquay area. Pee finished, and I was hot-footing it out of the loo when I noticed a couple of the human rodents who constitute Her Majesty's press loitering over by the washbasins looking very alert indeed.

I didn't give it any thought until just now, when I opened up today's papers to see a lot of rot along the lines of "England selection lottery – now Lord Ted sings Devon's praises". Flunky after flunky from the Board is now demanding to know why I've anointed this Malcolm Devon as England's new fast-bowling spearhead, so I said I barely knew the chap and it was all a terrible mix-up.

However, what with the rebel tours and whatnot, apparently we can't afford another "PR catastrophe" (not my words) so this Malcolm Devon will lead our attack tomorrow whether I like it or not. Well, I am not one to dampen a player's confidence by letting him know that he's only been selected due to an overheard misunderstanding in the lav, so I went straight up to Mr Devon and shook his hand. And after the Belgian Minister for Overseas Trade and Development had confirmed that he wasn't a right-arm quickie, but in fact a visiting dignitary here as a guest of the City of Nottingham, we all got on terribly well and I'm sure we'll give these Aussies a much better game in this Test.

Fart
of
Darkness

BOWL

MAN HOWL

AND OTHER POEMS

FRED TRUEMAN

NUMBER 11

Fred Trueman

Sydney First Test, day one, February 25th 1955
Given up on writing novel. Prose is for sneering snobs
in committees and comfortable seats. Only verse can be
true and real, like the truth of digging coal out word by
choking word. The truth of hitting a stripy hat batsman
above the heart with the bouncer.

Wrote this today about Hutton:

> *Professional*
> *Yorkshire*
> *Batsman*
>
> *Your strokes painting the*
> *glory but not on a church ceiling for vicars*
> *in long dresses like lasses*
>
> *Or bored souls in their Sunday*
> *best but for the taste of a*
> *pint*
> *after a day in the pit or a girl called*
> *Veronica with strong arms and a fondness*
> *for fast men*
>
> *Painted not by committee but by you alone*
> *and it made me*
> *sing*

And they called you captain and I were
proud to call you that too
Not because you went to Cambridge
University or your dad were someone
And they called you "professional"
like it were to say an insult like
"medium pacer" or "southern"

But I called you skipper

Until you fined me for unprofessional
behaviour on a tour of West Indies and
you were dead to me then and never again
would I call you captain for England and
there is nothing left of you to me now

And when they bowled you out for six
today I laughed and I wished it were me.

* * *

BOWL MAN HOWL

The boots and the hair and
the running running running
Good thick legs
And a boot full of blood
it were wasted
on thee.

Ian Bell

Perth, December 16th 2010

Hello?

Hello?

Hi, this is Ian Bell and I'm writing my diary with my new voice recognition software which is probably the most significant technological invention since the Gray Nicolls Scoop and listens to the words and types them out on the screen as you speak them. Erm. Obviously it was just nice to get some runs and hopefully I can kick on from here tomorrow and help the team post a really big sco—

Hang on. There's someone at the door. Oh hi, Swanny. No. No, I'm doing my diary. No, on the computer. Hang on, computer. Sorry. Oh wait, I don't have to say sorry, do I, you're not a human person. Wait, you're still typing. You can stop now. Seriously. Stop. Please STOP NOW. Oh. Help. No, Swanny, I can't come out this evening, thanks all the same. I've got to do my diary. Yeah. Yeah. On the computer.

Oh crikey, it's still typing. Swanny, make it stop. You know about cameras and computers and stuff. It's not funny, Swanny. It's like a machine taking over my mind like in *Terminator* or that documentary with Keanu

Reeves when he's got the long coat and we're all living in a computer game and not a good one like *Championship Manager* or something neither. It knows too much, Swanny. It knows everything. Swanny, do you think it can see into my soul like they said Jesus can in church? Does it know about the pictures of Rachel from S Club 7 hidden under the bed in the *Special Book of Batting Techniques and Tips* that Mr Goochie gave all of the batting unit? Oh God, it hears everything, Swanny. Delete that, don't type it down. Oh Jesus, what is mum going to say? Okay, hang on. I've got an idea. We'll fool it, Swanny.

Erm.

Yes, this is Ian Bell doing his diary and obviously it was disappointing to get out today having got a good start but on the other hand there was a lot of positives to take from the situation and I definitely haven't got any rude pictures under the bed or anything like that.

I think it bought it. Let's get out of here, Swanny.

Swanny? Shh. Quietly.

Back away slowly, Swanny. It's clever. Let's get out of here and meet the lads down in the bar area and let off a bit of steam but in the context of behaving in a professional manner. And then, once I figure out how to turn it off, I'm never using that computer again.

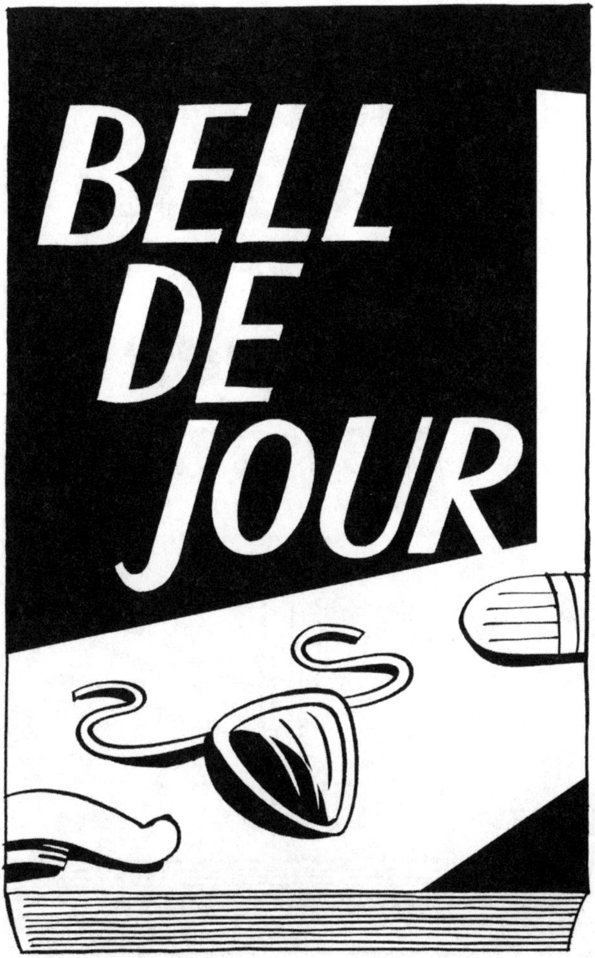
BELL
DE
JOUR

à la recherche du recherche du temper perdu

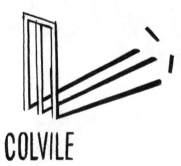

COLVILE

Charles Colvile

Sky Studios, Isleworth, December 19th 2010

5:15 PM

We've got a serious problem: Bob's in a really good mood. How the hell are we going to do *The Verdict* tonight? I ran into him in the corridor and he greeted me like a long-lost brother. Normally he just sniffs at me, says "milk and two" and mutters about the one-way system or how hard it is to get a decent custard cream these days. I need him grumpy, I need him mean, and I need him chuntering about the youth of today and their disgraceful over rates. Frankly, that's the stuff that's paying my mortgage, and, after all, an internationally famous television presenter has a certain standard of living to maintain.

5:35 PM

Have discovered why Bob is in such good spirits: he's finally won his court injunction to have all memorabilia with the slogan "Botham's Ashes" changed to "Botham AND Willis' Ashes". Apparently the Headingley 1981 market is worth "enough in DVD sales alone to stick another wing on Chateau Willis." Then he roared with laughter and dug me in the ribs in a matey way with one of those great big sharp knobbly pointy elbows. It was like being stabbed with a carving knife.

6:45 PM

This is seriously bad. Need to get Bob in a vile temper before we go on air. I snuck into his dressing-room and replaced all his Dylan CDs with One Direction; he just smiled and said "not as bad as *Shot Of Love*, at least".

6:55 PM

I got Rob Key to impersonate a journalist and phone Bob to ask if he would "agree that Steve Harmison was the best English fast-bowler since John Snow." He saw through it straight away. I told Rob to finish eating that Scotch egg before he called Bob, but would he listen? Bloody amateurs.

7:58 PM

Cracked it! Told Bob that the bigwigs wanted to take *The Verdict* in a less negative, less confrontational direction and that it was being replaced with a segment called *Knighty Knight*, where the cuddly ODI specialist gives you both sides of every story in an especially soothing and even-handed manner.

8:01 PM

On air, and Bob's in off the long run! He has just suggested that Steve Finn is a medium pacer, he'd like to see Andrew Strauss flayed alive for not having a fourth slip and threatened to make a citizen's arrest of Stuart Broad for crimes against length bowling. We're back, baby. Back!

Graham Gooch

Brisbane, January 20th 1991

Had a lie-in, so it was gone 4:45 AM when I got up to do my usual morning routine – five-mile jog, rigorous self-flagellation with a treasured old pair of Keith Fletcher's long johns and a round of hair regrowth exercises.

I was just coming down into the hotel lobby for breakfast – two litres of warm water with bits of raw turbot (protein), birdseed (carbs/essential oils) and daffodil (moustache thickener/naughty treat) in it – when I saw Gower. I was pleased to note that he was up and dressed, for once at a decent hour. He was in a black suit and white shirt combo; some toff fashion statement I suppose, but at least he was awake and ready for an important day.

A tour match against a State side is an ideal opportunity for some really serious "nets in the middle" as I call them, and I want Gower giving 125%. I had no time to talk, there being a four-hour net and a half-marathon to complete before play against Queensland, and as Fletch is fond of saying: the devil makes wafty waves outside off-stump for idle hands to do. Nodded at Gower, bench pressed (three sets of ten reps) a medium-sized occasional table in the lobby, and headed to restaurant.

Pleasing about Gower. Maybe I am finally getting through to him: there is simply no substitute for hard work and discipline, in cricket or in life.

David Gower

Brisbane, January 20th 1991

Slightly awkward moment just now: I had been at a black tie do with Prince Andrew – who is over here doing something or other on behalf of the good old British taxpayer – and we ended up "liberating" a submarine and taking it for a bit of a spin around Brisbane Harbour. Quite fun, although Andy may or may not have torpedoed a couple of smallish yachts.

I probably ought to have steered as HRH had most definitely had a few, but he insisted and, well, a prince is a prince, isn't he? Fortunately, he had some top-level contacts at the Foreign Office so we were able to smooth things over and emerge unscathed and un-incarcerated in time for a final glass of something cold and acceptable at the Admiral's place overlooking the harbour.

I was just easing myself back into the hotel when I saw the ridiculous slave-driver Gooch in the lobby, no doubt off for some nocturnal weight training. For a horrible moment, I thought he was going to make me do some cricket practice, but he stomped away and I glided up to bed for a few hours' shut-eye.

There's some pointless tour match later – a prospect which would normally bore me to tears, but I have managed to procure a Tiger Moth plane in which to buzz the ground, so that should give the boys a laugh. I am optimistic that Mr Gooch will have a conniption fit.

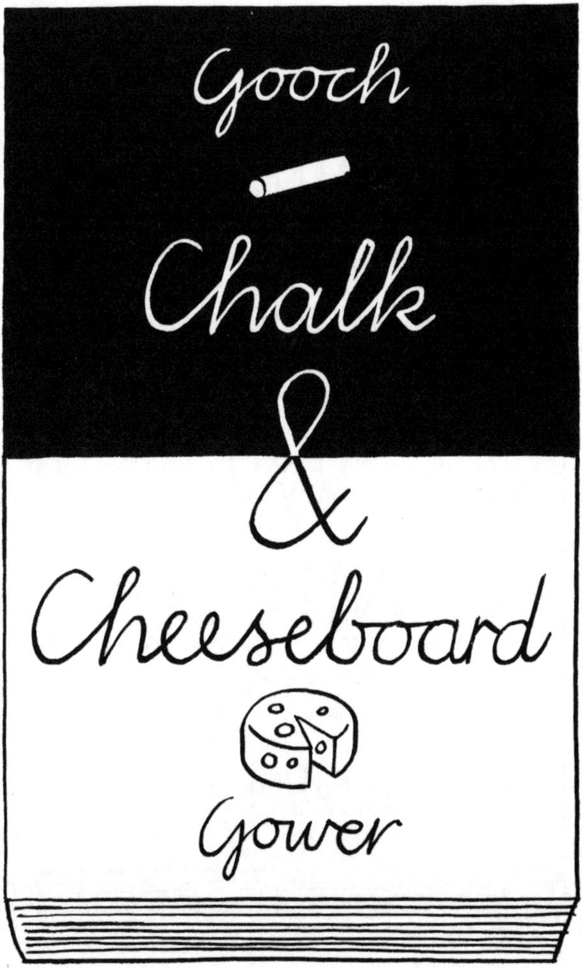
Gooch
Chalk
&
Cheeseboard
Gower

MIND
GAMES

Fletcher

Duncan Fletcher

Trent Bridge, August 27th 2005

Without doubt the most satisfying aspect of what I do is conceiving a plan, putting it into motion and then seeing the players execute it under the pressure of the live match environment. The Ponting run-out today was the culmination of months of preparation.

In January, I had sent Gary Pratt to Australia to tail Ponting. I had Gary check into each hotel Ponting was staying at, and make sure Ponting saw him doing something unusual and memorable in each one. Ponting did not know Gary from Adam, but he sees a man screaming on a cell phone in the lobby in Perth; the same man talking to a pot plant in the spa area at Melbourne; and then again wearing a loud Hawaiian shirt and carrying a snowboard in the breakfast buffet at Sydney. And every morning, hospitality arrives to do Ponting's room: it is Gary in a chambermaid outfit. He only pops his head around the door for a second before saying: "Ay dios mio, I am forget clean towel." Importantly, he does not return. Ponting fancies he recognises this mannish, incompetent cleaner. But from where?

Ponting is a fine cricketer, but his powers of facial recognition are no better than moderate. And as he is a busy person who meets a lot of people, he cannot be certain these strange but essentially insignificant events are even the same man. But it starts to nag at him.

By the spring, we are ready to step up the plan. I suggest to Gary that, while he has a lot of good qualities as a cricketer, no career lasts forever and he should consider other options. I persuade him to retrain as a hairdresser and he takes a job at Romeo's barbers in Launceston. Sure enough, Ponting is back home in March visiting his folks and he needs a haircut. Who's giving him a short-back-and-sides? A very familiar-looking guy from somewhere he can't place. Unsettling.

Once they arrive in England, we get to phase three. Ponting is a big watcher of DVDs on tour. We know from our research that he is a creature of habit: *GoodFellas*, *Babe: Pig in the City* (interestingly, he does NOT care for the original *Babe*) and *A Weekend at Bernie's*. Only these three. We have our video department recut these films, adding in a single frame – just 1/24 of a second – every now and then: an extreme close-up of Gary screaming. We obtain Ponting's DVDs and replace them with the doctored versions. Subliminally, Gary is right inside Ponting's head. Every time Ponting watches one of his films, a sense of disorientation and confusion results.

So today, Ponting is set and batting well. I instruct Gary to field in place of Simon Jones, telling him to get in Ponting's eye-line. At the end of the 43rd over, on my signal, he wanders up to Ponting and mutters: "Just a trim, is it, sir?" The penny drops – Ponting is distracted, his head's all over the place. Next over: bang, he's run out. No wonder he was furious. It just goes to show that you can't leave anything to chance at this level.

Donald Bradman

Leeds, July 11th 1930

Walked off the field at Headingley unbeaten on 309. Asked team-mates if they had enjoyed my innings. Apparently, there was a risk of sunstroke on the balcony so they all had to sit in the back room with the curtains drawn and not watch me bat at all. They were very sad to miss my knock, they said. Peculiar: it felt very overcast in the middle? Leeds has very localised weather, they explained.

Back at the hotel, they asked me to come to the bar for a drink – it being tradition for a century-maker to buy a round for the team. I acted quickly, as quickly as I do when using my feet to a spinner: I said I had lost my wallet. They did not believe me. I said I would go and get it from my room, then. Fled through kitchens. Hid in a dumb waiter until bar closed and they had all gone to bed.

Spent remainder of the evening in my room alone. Managed to fashion a primitive ball out of a couple of pairs of tightly rolled-up socks, which I then hardened by dipping in hair pomade and drying on the radiator. Practised bouncing this off the corner of bathroom sink and playing it with toothbrush for five hours. Scored an unbeaten 965.

July 12th

Awoke in middle of the night troubled by unfinished practice at Sockit. Got up approx four o'clock and played until toothbrush broke. Sat quietly in dark until breakfast, thinking about how to convert Headingley 309* into significant score.

July 14th

Still utterly disheartened about throwing wicket away on 334, although some good news on the sunstroke front at least. When I was dismissed, the fellows gathered on the balcony to clap and cheer. I noticed some champagne being opened. I asked about the sunstroke risk but apparently it had got cloudier that very minute. Thank goodness! Funny thing is, I don't drink champagne, and I told them as much. "We know," they said.

July 15th

Tomorrow we journey from Leeds to Durham for a tour match. My employers (Pongo Patterson & Sons Sporting Goods, Sydney) are laying on a small aircraft for me; my team-mates are going via omnibus (roof of). I wondered if they minded me travelling separately. "Oh no," they said. "We're just sorry to miss out on you talking us through every single ball of your innings again." Retire to room early to practice exercising my eyelid muscles for maximising light intake during murky conditions in North East. Do 2,000 shuttle runs in bathtub. Bed.

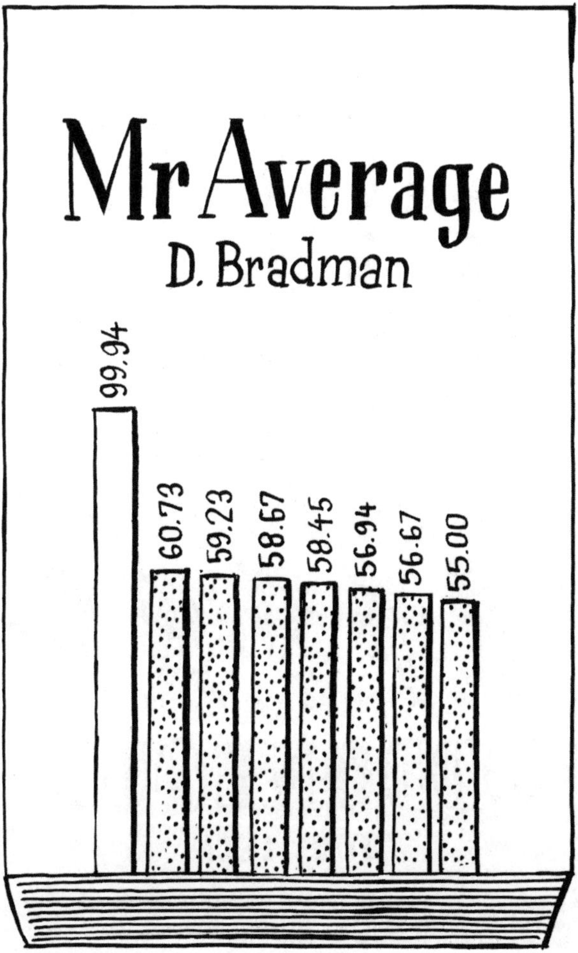
Mr Average
D. Bradman
99.94
60.73
59.23
58.67
58.45
56.94
56.67
55.00

ODDONEOUT

TONY LOCK

Tony Lock

Old Trafford, July 27th 1956
Good day for England. We've a lead of 406 still on first innings and the Australians are already one down. Laker got it; Colin McDonald nicely caught by yours truly. You're welcome, chummy. I should have had at least two leg-befores, a stumping, and any number of half-chances past slip, but I suppose I was happy enough to see Jim have his bit of success. It'll be my turn tomorrow, I'm sure.

Old Trafford, July 28th
G.A.R. Lock 14 overs, 3 maidens, 1 for 37
J.C. Laker 16.4 overs, 4 maidens, 9 for 37
What a fluky beggar. Nine bleeding wickets in all, and every one of them a result of my hard work and his good fortune. The turning-point was without doubt me getting rid of Burke, with His Majesty Cowdrey deigning to pouch the catch. Of course, after I'd kicked the door open, old Jim rushed through. Seven wickets for eight to wrap the innings up? What a show-off. And who's at the other end, setting them up like a slow-left arm barmaid? Muggins here.

We asked the Australians to follow on, so there was just time for a quick cup of tea in the dressing-room. I get in there, and guess who's had the last of the good sandwiches? Nancy Nine-Fer. He comes over, all friendly like, and you know what he has the cheek to say? "Great spell at the other end there, Tony. Here, I saved you the last of the cheese and pickle, mate." He knows fine well that I'm an egg and cress man, the selfish sod.

Old Trafford, July 29th
Rest day. Boring. But at least Laker didn't get any bloody wickets. My wickets.

Old Trafford, July 30th
Rained almost all day so stayed in the dressing-room. Played pontoon. Lost half my match fee to Laker. I don't think he even knows how to play the game: he twisted and hit 19, time and time again. Let's just hope he's used up all his luck before tomorrow.

Old Trafford, July 31st
G.A.R. Lock 55 overs, 30 maidens, 0 for 69
J.C. Laker 51.2 overs, 23 maidens, 10 for 53
Jammy bastard.

Merv Hughes

Australia, January 11th 2010
Been approached by some of the blokes at Tourism Australia to do a television commercial about foreigners coming to our country. They are pro it.

These advertising types, I tell you what, they make young Michael Clarke look like Keith Stackpole. It's Blackberry this and trendy glasses that and they talk more shit than a roomful of Pom cricket commentators moaning about the spirit of the game. I wouldn't be surprised if a couple of them were metrosexuals. There was a long speech about brand awareness that I managed to sleep through, and they were red-hot keen on something called synergy, which I was more or less certain was one of those fizzy drinks the young bowlers are so keen on these days.

They told me a key problem with marketing Australia is our self-image as a country and that "previous campaigns had been blindsided by cultural cringe". I said I know what you mean, all that arty-farty stuff makes me flaming sick as well.

March 9th
The advertising guys gave me some homework: think of a song for the advert that sums up what Australia means to you. Easy.

There's nothing like the sunrise
The first tinny of the day
Staring a Pommie in the face
And having plenty to say
There's nothing like Australia
Does your husband play cricket as well?
I'm going to knock your head off
Why don't you go to hell?
There's nothing like Australia
You little Pommie poof
I'll bowl you a piano
Let's see if you can play that
There's nothing like Australia
We've got Sheilas
And tashes
And beer
There's nothing like Australia
You're out
You Pommie queer
There's nothing like
Au-stray-li-aaaahh
There's nothing like
Austray-li-ahhhh

They're very pleased with me at the agency. I've been promoted to Head of Creative, and we start shooting the advert next month.

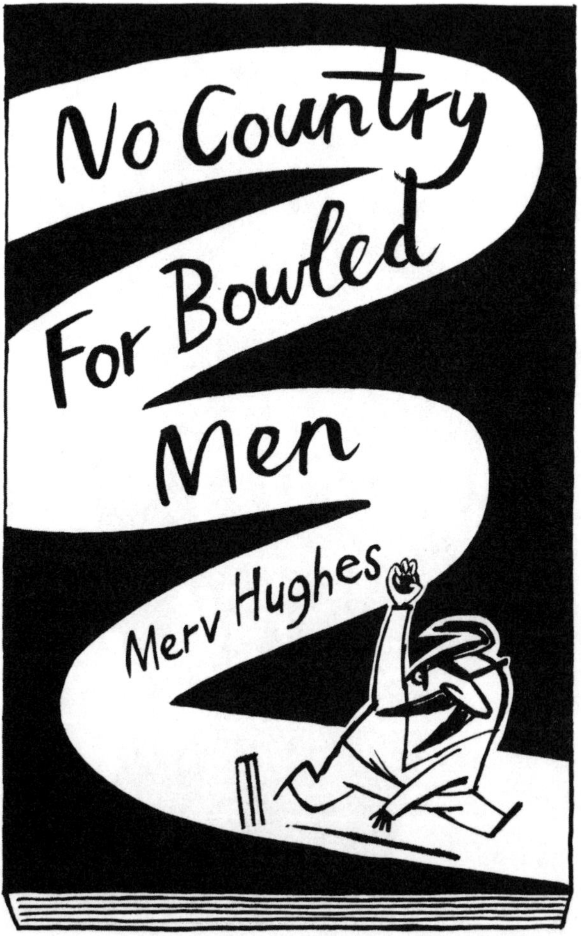
No Country
For Bowled
Men
Merv Hughes

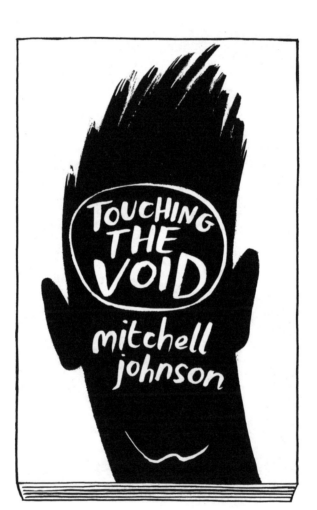

Mitchell Johnson

Melbourne, December 26th 2010

Hot.

Shouting.

Mr Ricky angry. Bowl ball on stumps he ask. Jeez mate for crying out loud try to get it on the stumps. Mitch trying! Why shouting always? Why must swearing words? Jeering, shouting, bowling. Hotness comes on back of neck and the sad thing inside. Mitch can has isotonic sports drink and rest on boundary? No. More bowling. Mitch sad. Always they make bowling.

Old man who makes shapes with arms makes long arm shape (both arms) say "WIDE" loud in Mitch ear. Mr Ricky cursing. Bad swears. Worse: Mitch must do another bowl as punishment. Where is cooling breeze and bouncy bouncy of nice Perth? Mitch have hatful! Stick it up Pommies! I am Mitch: hear me roar!

But this not Perth. Is one of the Other Places. The bad places. No breeze, no bouncy. Mitch worry, cannot focus on skill sets. Run up, do bowl. Smash Pommie stumps and the cheering and pats on bottom? Oh no. Arm naughty. WIDE. Good leaping Brad Haddin! Brad Haddin leap like Skippy the Bush Kangaroo but even still cannot stop ball. Ball run over rope behind Brad Haddin. Mr Ricky head in hands. Is head hurt? Mitch find aspirin pill for Mr Ricky? Poor Mr Ricky. No. Not headache. Just angry. Swearing.

New tattoo hurt. Hurt very bad, stings and burns. Mr Pigeon gave Mitch beer and beer and beer and they all chant drink drink drink. Mitch woked up next day covered in tattoo. Thirsty. Head hurt. Not as much as tattoo on shoulder though. Tattoo says, "We're going to beat the Poms 5–0".

Is code? Ancient language of Aborigine peoples? Meaning unclear to Mitch.

But not because Mitch is stupid! Or cannot do readings! Mitch can read just fine thank you. Mitch not stupid, Jessica attractive girlfriend of Mitch said so, you are not stupid Mitch don't listen to your mother she is trying to control you shout shout shout mother get out of my head leave my wrist position alone.

Tattoo hurting and old man with stretchy out arms is shouting "wide" and Mr Ricky has both hands on hips double teapot. Click heels three times and be back in Perth? Close eyes and wish very hard there's no place like home. But mother is at home! Mother shouts. She is here? Mother is here? No. Is in head. Calm calm calm focus wrist. Soon bowlings be over, then lunch comes. Cheese sandwich? Yes. Mitch calmer now. Focus on sandwich, execute plans.

Geoffrey Boycott

Yorkshire, April 3rd 2011

Ran into Bob Willis. He was listening to Bob Dylan on one of those iPod nonsenses. You can damage your hearing, I told him.

I first met Dylan when he came to watch me get an hundred on a seaming pitch at Scarborough in 1966. He asked me for a couple of tips and I told him my door's always open. He were a nice lad. I liked his ladyfriend too, Joan Baez, nice girl, good player, knows when to keep her mouth shut. Dylan was having some problems with his technique so I suggested to him that he should think about his head position and, if that didn't work, go electric.

I worked with him in the nets at Old Trafford on the Friday and he said he'd give it a go at the Manchester Free Trade Hall the next evening. I played drums: I didn't mind Dylan getting the limelight, I was never that sort of player. The crowd were right on his back, as bad as I've seen, worse than when I got an important 63 not out against the Aussies at Brisbane earlier that winter.

Anyway, Dylan started out with a lot of rubbish, acoustic stuff, and I shouted to him from behind the drum kit: "*Visions Of Johanna* – absolute roobish, my mother could play that wi' a stick of rhubarb." He was mad as anything and he yelled back: "I don't believe you, you're a liar," and then he whispered that he reckoned

Raymond Illingworth were twice the captain that I'd ever be.

That was like a corkscrew in my heart. I shouted out "Judas" and got the hell off the stage. We didn't speak for some time after that but we did patch things up later in Mozambique, where I've got a holiday home. I took Brian Close out there one spring, but Closey never rated Dylan much; he always preferred Woody Guthrie.

Looking back, there's no doubt in my mind that going electric were the best thing Dylan could have done and I'm glad I told him to do it. A few years later, he repaid the favour: I was having some problems against Jeff Thomson and I went to see Dylan in Nashville. He suggested getting back and across, covering the off stump. "The ghost of electricity is howling down your corridor of uncertainty, man," he said to me. I worked on it in the nets and ended up getting an hundred against the Aussies at Headingley. He had a funny way of talking, but I respected him and I know he thought a lot of me. Great player, but of course he never had to play on uncovered pitches.

The Unbearable Rightness of Being

GEOFFREY BOYCOTT

Ricky Ponting

Melbourne, December 28th 2010

Not a good couple of days. Getting into it with Andrew Strauss and Aleem Dar was bad enough, then this morning I agreed to do a personal appearance for one of the charities I support. It went pretty ordinary, if I'm honest. I'm very proud to be a patron of Squinters-R-Winners. It does a lot of great work with kids who have serious squints and teaches them there's no reason they can't go all the way to the very top. But that might be in jeopardy now, thanks to the pen-pushers.

We'd arranged for some of the kids to come to the MCG for the Test but a lot of parents felt it would be too upsetting for them to have to watch Australia play cricket. I'd be lying if I said that made me feel good. We managed to fix something up short notice before play at a McDonalds nearby the G where the poor little squinters could have some burgers, I'd do a bit of a coaching session and then Ronald McDonald would do some magic tricks or whatever it is they like.

I thought it might be a good chance to bat myself into a bit of form but I tell you what, you underestimate these squinty kids at your peril. I had a bat, and after getting beaten by a couple of length balls from one of the girls first up, I was starting to feel the pressure. Next ball, I see it early and I'm back in the crease looking to swivel pull, but it gets big on me and I have to drop the hands. I swear on my life I've never got a touch on it, but I'm caught at third slip by Hamburglar and all the little bastards are going wild.

I say, "Aw look," and stand my ground, as is my right. But I can't believe it – Ronald McDonald's got his big clown finger right up in the air and he's sawn me off stone dead. I try to reason with him say, "Come on mate, I was nowhere near it." Meanwhile Hamburglar's right up in my grille giving me the big send-off. I start to lose the rag and I say, "I want a bloody video review."

Ronald McDonald goes, "Well you're in luck mate, because we had to have CCTV put in after Shane Warne came here to film that advert and we caught him trying to steal four metric tons of McNuggets for personal use." He gets some security bloke to look at the tape and they're all saying I hit it fair dinkum. Ronald McDonald says, "Look at that Hotspot on your bat," and I say, "That's not Hotspot, that's effing ketchup, what are you bloody kidding me?"

Anyway, long story short, I'm up before Mayor McCheese for dissent and that's another half a match fee down the swanny. Those little squinters are on their own now, and as far as I'm concerned, it serves them right.

Rod Marsh

Secret location, July 27th 2001

This diary will serve as a record of my time as director of the English national academy and will be read only by myself and my handler back in the Australian Cricket Board. No names, no pack drill, but he goes by the top-secret codename AB. If you're reading, AB mate, g'day.

Spent first few weeks establishing my cover for Operation Destroy The England Cricket System From Within. Still find it hard to believe that Poms have installed me right at the heart of their organisation. This could be the biggest espionage victory since we managed to flip Craig White and use him as a triple agent in their fast bowling unit.

April 16th 2002

Issued a statement saying how proud I was to be working for the Poms and describing myself as a "100% English supporter now". Being this deep undercover can start to mess with your mind – and of course you lose a lot of mates. Dennis Lillee sent me a barbequed dingo's toe in the mail, the traditional Western Australia Cozzy Nostra warning for a suspected traitor. That hurt.

May 25th 2004

I have trained and reprogrammed a young fast bowler from Lancashire called Sajid Mahmood. Operation

Mancunian Candidate will see me able to detonate the brainwashed subject remotely from the safety of the pavilion. On my signal, he will unleash a wild display of inaccurate filth that could undermine the English seam effort for years to come. He is scheduled for deployment in the 2006–07 Ashes.

June 4th 2005
Completing my sabotage work on wicketkeepers. Chris Read is excellent but, for whatever reason, Duncan Fletcher is determined to burn this asset. Are the Zimbabweans also trying to come to the party and make their mark in international spy games? Intriguing. Aussie patriot Geraint Jones is doing some excellent undercover work with the gloves.

August 18th 2005
Seriously concerned that the Poms have flipped Agent Troy Cooley. His English bowlers are going gangbusters this summer. Tried to slip him a message in a can of XXXX on the balcony, but he said he was too busy motivating Harmison. Can't work out if he's a double agent, or if he's a triple agent, or if I'm a double triple, or if I've been working for Fletcher's internal affairs bureau all along. Better extract myself back to the Motherland for debriefing.

Message ends.

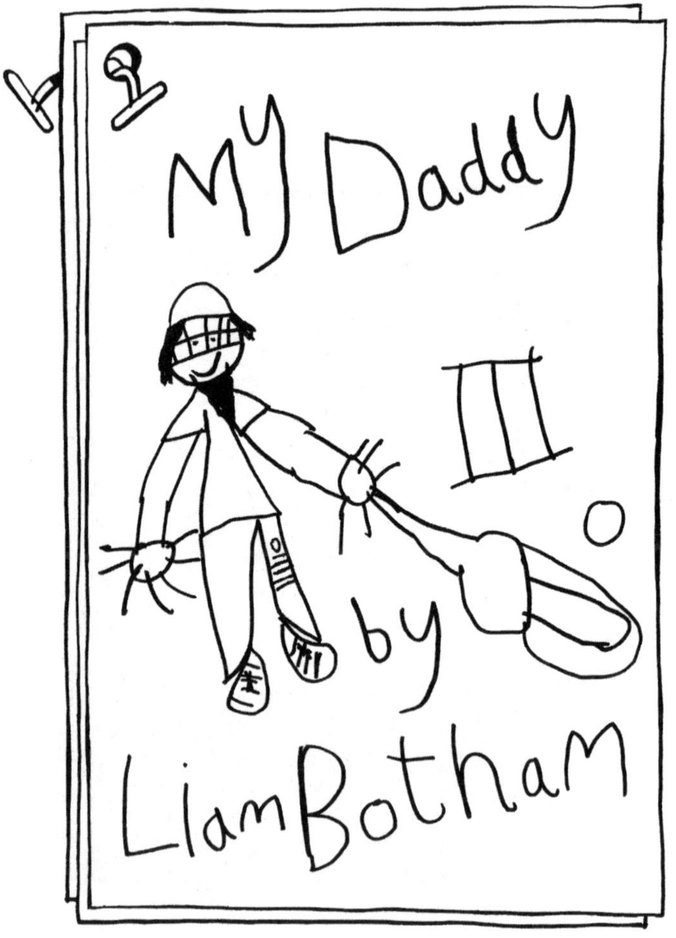

My Daddy
by
Liam Botham

Liam Botham
St Gilbert's Infant School

Headingley, July 21st 1981

Daddy had a big partie for all his frends today becoz they wun in crikit becoz of Daddy. Daddy all ways wins in crikit. We play crikit in the gardin and I bol at Daddy for owers and owers and Daddy all ways hits the ball for miles and miles and it is my speshal job to go and fech it. And bol it agen. So Daddy can hit it agen. Sumtims I get tired out but Daddy sez we can not stop becoz all the boling and feching is gud for bilding my strenf of carikter.

At the partie ther woz a juggla and a majishun to keep the boys and girls inturtayned. But Daddy gotted into a compatishun wiv the juggla and betted the juggla that he cud juggul mor balls than wot the juggla cud. The juggla did 6 balls but then Daddy dropted wun of his balls wen he wuz jugguling. But Daddy sed it was obfeeus that the juggla had been cheeting and doing sumfing called tampuring wiv the balls and there woz an argyumen and the juggla had to leev.

We liked the majishun mor betta than the juggla becoz the majishun cud do triks like soring a laydy in harf and making a bunyrabit come owt of his hat. Daddy arsked the majishun if the majishun cud make baloon animals and the majishun sed shor of cors he cud and he cud do making a pussycat an a horssy an a moocow an a baa lamb an also he cud make a speshal baloon crown for speshal boys and girls to wear. Daddy got reely mad abowt the speshal baloon crown for speshal boys and girls becoz he sed it woz dissrespekful to Her Majisty The Kween and he stompt off but the majishun karmd efreewun down and made us happy by making a bunyrabit come owt off Daddy's eer!!

Daddy sed to the majishun that anywun cud do that trik too but it turnds owt that the majishun must of dun sumfing norty becoz wen Daddy tryd to do the trik he cudnt make the bunyrabit com owt of the hat or from behind his eer or anyfing. Daddy sed to the majishun "Wel how many Test wikkits hav you got then?" and the majishun did not hav an arnser to that.

The majishun orso had a very pritty laydy wiv him hoo woz corled a majishun's asistunt and the majishun sed that the laydy cud do sord swallering and Daddy sed "I bet she can" but the majishun herd this an gotted very cross an efreewun sed it mite be for the best if you left mate and so the majishun pakkd up his fings and went away and that was the end.

Shane Warne

Las Vegas, November 25th 2010

I'm not one of those ex-players to sit on commentary bagging the blokes out there doing their best, but sometimes I have to admit I'm tearing my hair out (although obviously, thanks to my good friends at Advanced Hair Studios, the old Warnie mop has plenty to spare).

I see a guy like young Xavier Doherty and I think to myself: "Jeez Louise, this kid needs some work." To be a top-rate spin bowler you need a good solid action, you need a bit of variation and you need some endorsements from local businesses. Nobody's expecting a young feller making his way in the game to be pulling in the sponsorship deals from your 888poker.coms or your McDonaldses – as I said to myself only this morning while eating a Chicken McFlurry and enjoying an online gambling experience that's second to none – but there's just not the commercial hunger that we had when we were starting out.

I heard on the grapevine that Xavier hasn't even got his own range of underwear yet, and it's sad if that's the guidance he's getting from Cricket Australia. There's so much potential there for Xavier as a male intimates brand – XL, X For Men, a racy XXX range for the man who thinks that little bigger. But no, he's happy in a pair of tighty-whities from Target or whatever. If you don't do the simple things like trousering a few bucks from a line of signature undercrackers, how are you going to perform when the pressure's on and there's an Indian television channel on the phone asking you for your best price on a three-advert deal and a chat show?

Melbourne, December 26th
I'm happy to advise on affairs of the heart, not just affairs of the wallet, and I know Nathan Hauritz is very down about not getting in the team. I said to him, you've got to put yourself in the front of the selectors' minds, make it impossible for them to ignore you. So I've told him to get into some Twitter banter with an internationally famous megababe and take it from there.

Sydney, January 2nd 2011
Young Mike Beer came to see me after getting the nod for the SCG and we did a few exercises. Finger strength and speed is really important, so I told him to get his phone out and text a couple of stock phrases: "Hey babe – cant wait to get hot at yr hotel l8r!! xxxx" and "Aw look, sorry Liz, I've never seen that woman b4 in my life fair dinkum xx" but to be brutally honest I don't reckon Beero has got the fingering skills you need to be a top player. Sad, but there you have it.

Andrew Flintoff

Sydney, December 30th 2006

Another huge barney with Fletcher over selection. It's New Year's Eve and he wants a choice of light beers and soft drinks for the party? I told him I want Sambuca, and plenty of it. And after what happened at cricket practice this morning, we'll probably need a fire extinguisher. If Monty can't muck in with the rest of the lads and put away his share of Flaming Ferraris, then maybe he needs to think about his commitment to the team. And that beard'll grow back in no time, I should reckon.

Also, we'll need some of them right big glasses with fruit and sparklers in them. And an ice sculpture in the shape of the Ashes urn, or maybe in the shape of the Red Bull logo, throw a bone to our good pals over there. And a crate of Newcastle Brown Ale for Harmy, to stop him getting too homesick.

I told Fletcher all this and he started muttering. I said to him: "Look, we're 4–0 down. Let's not throw the series away because you've let morale slip for the sake of some penny-pinching."

December 31st, 9:30 PM
The New Year's Eve party is just getting going. Vaughany's here, standing off to one side, sipping his dry white wine. Got a funny half-smile on his face; if I didn't know him better I'd think he looked a bit superior almost. He's said

throughout the tour he's not trying to stick his oar in, but he's here for tactical advice if I want it. I thought, sod it, so I asked him straight: should we start off with pin the tail on the donkey or go straight into a conga? "I think you should trust your judgment, Fred," he said and he gave me that odd smirk again.

11:45 PM
Seeing all them boats in Sydney harbour has give us an idea. Come on, shipmates!

January 2nd 2007
Missed out yesterday, but I've come up smiling today and am right looking forward to stuffing the Aussies in the final Test. We've prepared as well as any team possibly could have: Alka-Seltzer, black coffee, had a nice sit down with the *Daily Star* crossword (flown over special – nothing left to chance) in the khazi. Just got to check the open-top bus is booked to take us round Sydney after the match and we're golden.

C.B. Fry

The Oval and elsewhere, August 14th 1905

Rise early, and sprint down to Hove for my morning swim. I am so preoccupied translating the works of Ovid into Hungarian in my head that I swim too far. It appears I have reached Morocco, and – as it turns out – in world-record time. The natives appear pleased to see me and insist that I am some species of deity. I decline modestly, telling them that I am (contrary to appearance) a mere mortal. After a diverting hour teaching various local worthies in Marrakech how to play golf, I run back to The Oval in time to score 144 against the Australians. During tea, I invent a clever device for communicating remotely with one's acquaintances while on the move. I name it the CB radio. Win world welterweight title, then home to bathe and dress for the evening, before dining with the ravishing Countess of Sexpotamia, whom I enchant with my fire-eating skills. Score.

London, August 22nd 1912

Disaster and calumny most foul! I am finished as a polymath and as a cricketer. At The Oval this morning, I completed 79 comfortable runs against the touring Australians before calamity struck. I was playing a game of chess with my good friend Emanuel Lasker over by the cover boundary between each delivery and then sprinting back to the crease as the bowler ran up to take my guard. Unfortunately, on 79, I slipped on the turf and tumbled in an undignified heap. I leapt to my feet, performing a triple somersault and dictating the correct method for solving world hunger as I did so in order to cover my faux pas, and returned to the bat.

Immediately I knew something was wrong, for I was caught by Jennings off the bowling of Hazlitt without further score. On returning to the pav, I felt in my trouser pocket for my lucky conker. My most treasured possession, it has been with me since a boy and is, I firmly believe, the source of all my power. I became frantic – it was nowhere to be seen. At close of play I searched for it hither and yon, crawling over The Oval outfield upon my hands and knees until well beyond nightfall in futile search for that tiny little withered nut that contains my life-force. I shall never play for England again.

Hove, June 23rd 1928
Still no conker. Go mad.

Rangoon, July 15th 1934
A telegram from Adolf Hitler, who say he may have found my conker. I make haste for Germany. Oh happy day! My conker is back!

Oxford, April 30th 1945
Suspect Adolf, although a capital fellow, may have lied about posting my conker. There is nothing left for me now but to work for the *Daily Express*.

THE FREUDIAN SLIP

JM BREARLEY
MA CANTAB

Michael Brearley

NOTES ON THE SUBJECT THOMSON, J.
First Test, Lord's, June 16th 1977
(*J.M. Brearley c Robinson b Thomson 9*)
I have a new patient: Jeff, a troubled young Australian man with behavioural difficulties. I asked him to come and see me at clinic in St John's Wood. He immediately sought to assert dominance with a threatening look and a volley of expletives. (Anger management issues? Possible Tourette's? Hangover?) I quickly deduced that it was important to establish his trust, which I did by edging one to slip and getting back to my study in the pavilion, better to explore some theories about the patient.

Second Test, Old Trafford, July 8th
(*J.M. Brearley c Chappell b Thomson 6*)
Further session with the patient. He greeted me, as has become our custom, with a torrent of bad language centred around my mother, the marital status of my parents at the time of my birth and a suggestion that I am an enthusiastic masturbator. What dark secrets lie in Jeff's past to generate this well of sexualised animosity? "Oh nothing," he replied quite cheerfully. "I just hate stuck-up Poms." Clearly his walls of self-defence and denial are carefully erected and maintained. Sadly, our time was up, so I feathered one to the cordon and terminated our session without further breakthrough.

Fourth Test, Headingley, August 11th
(J.M. Brearley c Marsh b Thomson 0)

Only time for a very brief consultation today – but what progress! I encouraged the patient to free-associate, letting him know that he was in a completely safe space where he could just let his mind go and say whatever words came to him. "You arsehole, I'm going to shove this shitty bat up your poncy English arse, you dirty Pommie arsewipe," said Jeff. And then it struck me – the patient has obviously become fixated in the anal stage of development, beyond any doubt because of some deep trauma as a very young child. I was so excited that I immediately tickled one behind and retired to the pav to write up my notes.

Fifth Test, The Oval, August 30th
(J.M. Brearley c Serjeant b Thomson 4)

More field research and occupational therapy with the patient, who has made splendid process. "Morning Brearley, you dirty son of a bitch," said Jeff. I thought it was extremely interesting that he would choose to greet me in that way, and I put it to the patient that perhaps he was really expressing his anger and resentment at *his* mother? Unfortunately, we were unable to explore this more deeply as Jeff dismissed me almost immediately. I have decided to invite him to come and work with me at Middlesex, so we can continue our excellent progress on his therapy, and also so I won't have to bat against him anymore.

Henry Blofeld
Aged 9

England v Australia, The Oval, August 14th 1948
An absolutely splendid day at my first-ever Test. I was having tea at Simpson's-in-the-Strand with Nanny – do you know Nanny? – quite a formidable character and rather too firm about certain bedtime-related matters for my personal taste but a dear old thing nevertheless. Anyhow, the Jammy Dodgers at Simpson's were exquisite as per and, as I sat there sipping on a delightfully zesty orange squash of indeterminate yet recent vintage, I thought what could be more absolutely marvellous than a day at the cricket, and I said as much to Nanny. Nanny, quick as a flash, quipped, "If it gets you to shut up for more than five seconds then I'm all for it," and gave me a loving forearm smash to the face.

Before I knew it we were aboard the Number 3 bus en route to The Oval and what a super bus it is too. I entertained some of the passengers on the top deck with an impromptu sightseeing tour, and some of them enjoyed it so much they had to get off the bus in indecent haste. I expect they were so wrapped up in my descriptions that they quite forgot their stops, the poor things.

There was some initial confusion when we got to the ground and a ticket gentlemen appeared to require payment from Nanny and myself to allow us to enter. Naturally I said to him, "Look here, don't you know who

I am?" and suggested instead that, seeing as he had been enjoying the benefit of my company for several seconds already, it was rather *him* who ought to be paying *me*.

The matter was eventually sorted out satisfactorily, with the man dismissed from his employment and, according to Nanny, certain to be sent to gaol. We took our seats. The crowd was in a state of considerable excitement, being as Bradman had just walked out to bat and, with the dear old clock ticking round to six and the shadows lengthening, it was as thrilling an evening as you could wish for.

"I say, Nanny," I said. "Isn't this super? And my goodness me, here comes Lindwall, I mean Ranji, I mean I beg your pardon here comes Bradman and the score is, now let me see, 68–4, ah, 190–8, that is to say 117–1 and Compton needs just four runs for an average of 100.

"The nation of India, sorry, Tanganyika, no Warwickshire, I mean Australia, holds its breath as Hollies comes up to bowl with that familiar looping run of his and Bradman's done it! He's done it! He's hit him for four and… oh good gracious me, no. He's out! He's out! Bradman has been bowled second ball and, my, what a super pigeon over there at square leg, almost military in his bearing, wouldn't you say, Nanny?"

And, the rummest thing, I turned to Nanny and she had simply vanished from sight. I fancy I caught a glimpse of her later, positively tearing down the Harleyford Road, but I can't be sure. I wonder if I shall ever see her again.

HENRY

PORTRAIT OF A SERIAL FILLER

WILDEBEEST AT MID OFF
A Graphic Novel · Kevin Pietersen

Kevin Pietersen

The Oval, 12 September 2005

10:00 AM

Is Kevin Pietersen feeling the pressure? No way, buddy. No chance. He's thriving on it. And needing to bat to win the Ashes, that's not pressure. I'll tell you what pressure is: having a ridiculous quota system up your arse and not knowing where your next match fee is coming from. That's pressure.

So Fletcher comes up and tells me to get back in the crease, be patient, look to play Warne with the spin. Privately, I disagree – I'm going to get forward and attack him – but I'd never publicly challenge a coach or let it be known if I didn't share his views. It's not the way Kevin Pietersen goes about his business. Anyway, I might not even have to bat, and it's not about me: it's about the team.

LUNCH, 12:30 PM, ENGLAND 127–5

Wow. What a session. Dropped off Warne, and then dropped BY him off Lee. When you play against your best mate, it's a strange emotion – we're on opposite sides at the moment, but me and Warnie know we're going to be close for the rest of our lives. That's what you look for in the crazy world of professional sport: enduring relationships, not the quick buck and the bullshit of celebrity. Warnie understands. Only wish they would bring Michael Clarke or Simon Katich on instead: feel like I could bat against left-arm spin forever without getting out.

TEA, 3:10 PM, ENGLAND 221–7

An Ashes century. Not bad for a kid from Pietermaritzburg. Loving the applause. They like me! They really like me! Important thing now is to remember my mantra: don't do anything flashy, nothing premeditated, just stick to the basics. Kevin Pietersen will not be the sort of cricketing great who throws it away once he has got in. Wonder if I can hit a boundary standing on one leg while holding just the toe of the bat and potting the ball with the handle like it was a game of pool? NO. Later. Wait until my legend is assured.

EVENING, SOME TIME

What a feeling! This international cricket is a lot easier than they said.

Phil Tufnell

The Oval, August 23rd 1997
11 Aussie wickets in the match. Nice little result for
yours truly. Phone's been ringing day and night – some
agent geezer reckons there are plenty of opportunities
in showbiz for someone like myself. And first up, a
documentary is on the cards!

September 24th 1998
Filming on *Silly Mid Gaffe – Phil The Cat's Cricketing
Foul-Ups* is not going well. I told the producers my
vision for the film: a delicate, non-linear piece about the
existential futility of cricket as a metaphor for life itself,
but set on a kibbutz and with more lesbians. I saw *Gaffe*
as an oblique homage to Kieslowski's *Three Colours*
trilogy, in memoriam of dear Krzysztof. Instead, I am
sitting in a portacabin in Elstree pretending to guffaw
at a clip of David Lloyd being struck in the groin by Jeff
Thomson. When I saw the rushes of myself exclaiming,
"One ball left, eh Bumble?" I must confess that I nearly
packed it in there and then.

April 24th 2003
Agent has got me a role in *I'm A Celebrity... Get Me
Out Of Here*. Intriguing title. Is it, I asked, a painfully
poignant exploration of mental illness and the human
need for acceptance seen through the eyes of two

Polish transsexual dockyard workers in the era of Lech Walesa? He said not so much with the Polish ladyboys, but otherwise I was spot on. I fly to Australia tonight.

May 15th

Optimistic my triumph on the horrific *I'm A Celebrity* will finally provide me with the platform to get funding for the film I want to make. That I MUST make. *Down Blunder – 100 Ashes Cricket Rickets* will finally bury the outdated narrative conventions of Western cinema. It will be my *Seventh Seal*.

May 16th

A Question of chuffing *Sport*. That's what two weeks of eating maggots on live TV has brought me.

I am doomed forever to play a clown of the basest kind. This evening, I did an after-dinner speech in Chichester for the Worshipful Company of Double Glazers (Sussex). My agent has just telephoned to say they were dissatisfied. Philistines. I'd like to defenestrate the lot of them. What possible artistic purpose is served by 45 minutes of reheated anecdotes about Mike Gatting, a prawn vindaloo and a malfunctioning lavatory at Grace Road? Instead, I showed them a very challenging, very unique piece of interpretive dance reimagining *The Battle of Algiers* as a metaphor for a failed marriage that I developed during my stint as guest artistic director of the Rambert Dance Company. And I should give them back their money? I should have asked for double.

THE
'KING
SPEECH

JONATHAN TROTT

ONE MAN'S STRUGGLE
TO SPEAK WITH AN
ENGLISH ACCENT

Jonathan Trott

The Oval, August 23rd 2009

Boy, are we going to party tonight! As a youngster growing up in Cape Town, I never dreamed that I would one day be part of an Ashes-winning team. Like, really, not at all.

When I think about some of the okes I grew up playing with – Big Joost, Bakkies, Lekker Nantie, Mpumelele (known to one and all as Piet) and of course Hendrik Verwoerd (no relation) – well, if they could see me now! Obviously, if Joost and Bakkies get a result with the passport people then we could all be back playing together again as soon as England's next ODI series, but the point is: I've come a long way. When you've wanted something as badly as I've wanted an Ashes medal (I figure we probably get a medal?) for as long as I have, that's days and days of pent-up feelings and expectation, and I'm going to get stuck into the beers tonight like Jacques Kallis at an all-you-can-eat boerewors buffet.

August 24th

Hangover. I haven't been involved in a piss-up like that since ~~we~~ South Africa beat England at Edgbaston last summer (as they call August and the other winter months over here). Having spent many an evening at the Shepherd's Bush Walkabout on two-for-one Biltong Daiquiri nights, I thought I knew about drinking, but

Freddie Flintoff takes it to another level. He was talking at me for about 15 minutes before I realised he wasn't speaking Afrikaans. Still, it's not every year that you get to win the Ashes, is it? (Or is it? Better check this.) And Freddie reckons we might all get a CBE, which will be something to tell the folks back home.

August 25th
STILL feeling a bit rough, so I decide to have a special treat to cheer myself up: I take all my toiletries and line them up in rows, count them 27 times, and then arrange all the furniture in alphabetical order, then thematically and by size, and then finally scratch my left knee 2,056 times with my fourth most favourite loofah. Feel a bit calmer, so put in a bit of work on learning the words to the English national anthem, practise talking about the weather and how to look uncomfortable when people say nice things about me, then snatch a couple of hours kip before we all go to Ireland to play in an ODI.

Andrew Strauss

Sydney, January 7th 2011

"Can I get you anything else, skipper, or can I go and join in celebrating with the lads?"

I look up from my armchair in the corner of the dressing-room, feeling as happy with his lot as a chap who has just returned from a bumper day's shooting to find the Hon Georgina Muffington-Fruuli draped over his chaise longue wearing nothing but an alluring smile and a strategically positioned page of the *Financial Times* covering great news for pork belly futures.

"No, you go on, Cook," I say. "Just freshen up the old G&T and then you get out there and enjoy yourself."

"Thanks, skipper," says the faithful fellow. He does the necessary and I note, allowing myself a small flush of pride, that he has cut my slice of lime to precisely the right thickness. Flower is absolutely right: attention to detail can make all the difference.

"You know, I used to have a cook called Cook," I muse. "Are you by any chance related? Powerfully built woman, ruddy face, terribly good on puddings, especially the treacle varietals?"

"I don't *think* so, skipper," he says.

I say that I expect not, and dismiss him with a cheery wave. I fall into a reverie of satisfaction at a cricketing job jolly well done.

SOMETIME LATER

The dressing-room door is bundled open by a few of the chaps in a great flush of excitement.

"Skipper, come and have a go at t'Sprinkler," says Bresnan.

"Has Gardener not taken care of that?" I ask. "That wretched man, always smoking his roll-ups in the potting shed."

"It's a dance, skipper," explains Cook.

I must confess that the Strausses are not great dancers – although Great Aunt Macadamia Strauss did have a hand in inventing the Charleston – but a leader must muck in with the fellows where he can.

"A dance, eh?" I say. "Ought I to change into something a bit smarter?"

Cook assures me it is quite an informal affair and I think, why the devil not?

LATER STILL

Tired but happy after a long evening's celebration. I tuck Belly in, step over a snoring Bresnan, turn out the dressing-room lights and head to bed for a restorative eight hours. Tomorrow: the red-eye to Canberra for our eagerly awaited seventeen-match one-day series.

WHEN
THE
GOING
GETS
TOFF

Strauss

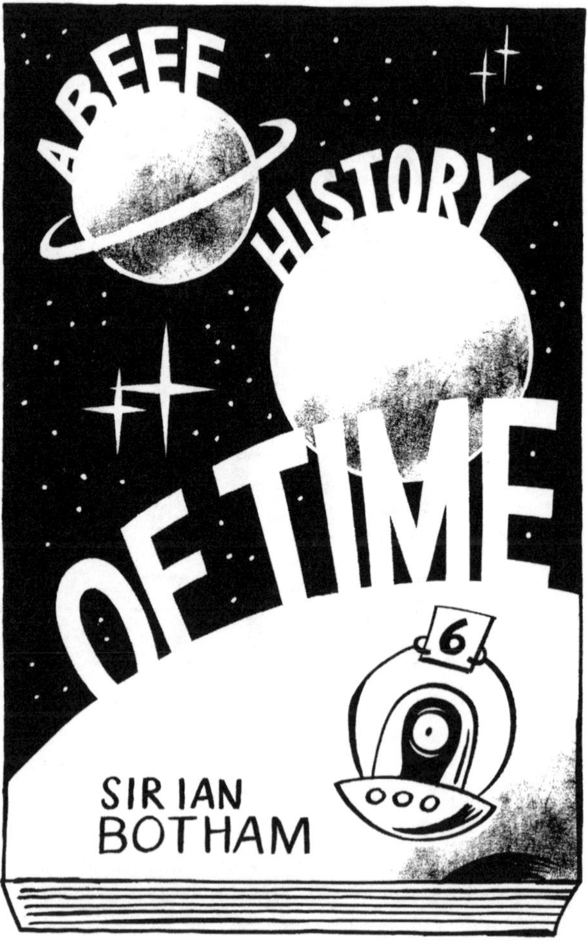
A BEEF HISTORY OF TIME
6
SIR IAN BOTHAM

Sir Ian Botham

Planet Headingley Carnegus X, Stardate 383, Year 2981

I just don't know what is going on out there. Can somebody explain to me how these players can claim to be tired, when they have been transported at light speed across the galaxy in suspended animation and then given three Carnegian lunar weeks to acclimatise to the oxygen-free atmosphere on this planet?

Bowlers get fit to bowl by bowling, not by teleporting themselves around the space–time continuum or having their hyperdrives tinkered with by so-called experts. When you see the ridiculous line-up of backroom droids, hundreds of them, it's no wonder these boys are getting mixed messages. I don't seem to remember Andy Roberts needing an antigravity accelerator or Bob Willis seeking advice from a vast supercomputer about line and length, and I honestly can't see that these players are really benefitting from so-called technology either.

You can prove anything with statistics, as I am always telling nerds like the Benedict B5000 Scorebot, so who cares if the numbers say that averages are getting better? Correct me if I'm wrong, but this game is all about who goes out there, in space, and performs on the day and one thing I can guarantee you is this: these Austrayloborgs won't be giving up just because their planet's tumbled into a supernova causing the total destruction of this entire arm of the galaxy.

As for the field placings, well, I'm sorry, but it's just a joke. I simply can't understand why there are not one, not two, but three drones hovering over on the lunar side of the planet, and then an enormous gap here where the force field should be. I would be putting a laser-powered warp defence pike here, and an unimaginably powerful death star here, here, here, and here, and giving the Austrayloborgs something to think about.

You can talk all you want about modern methods and the rest of it, but even though I've been a cryogenically preserved head in a jar for over 950 years now, I'd still fancy a bowl against some of that lot out there. The techniques look very ordinary indeed, and I think it's because they lack the mental strength we had. The latest buzz word is telekinesis: well, I was moving stuff with my mind back in 1977, and I didn't have to pick at the seam with a bottle top to do it. Or use an electron ram.

Today, it's all invisible force fields and jet-packs to get you through your delivery stride, and is the game any better for it? Viv Richards didn't need to be powered with infinitely dense dark matter from the heart of the sun, and I don't see why these modern players should be either. Sometimes, I think that they won't be happy until the players are all robots and that will be a great, great shame.

BY THE SAME AUTHORS

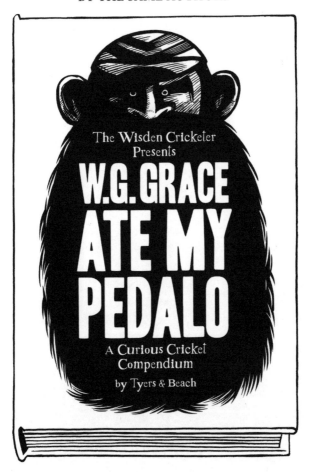